MY FIRST ENCYCLOPEDIA

An eye-catching series of information books designed to encourage young children to find out more about the world around them. Each one is carefully prepared by a subject specialist with the help of experienced writers and educational advisers.

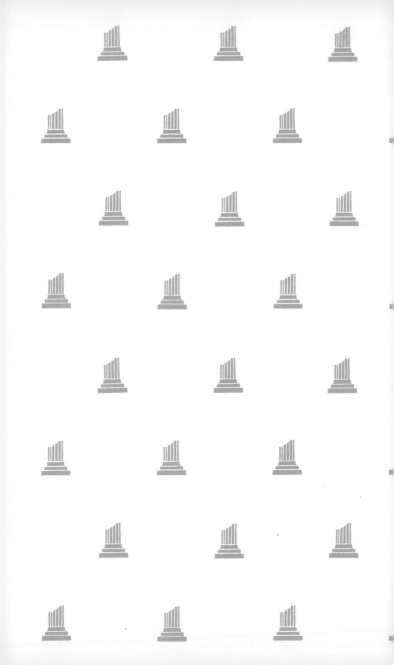

KINGFISHER
Kingfisher Publications Plc
New Penderel House, 283-288 High Holborn, London WC1V 7HZ

First published in paperback by Kingfisher Publications Plc 1994
2 4 6 8 10 9 7 5 3 1

1BP/0500/SF/(FR)/135MA

Originally published in hardback under the series title Young World
This edition © copyright Kingfisher Publications Plc 2000
Text & Illustrations © copyright Kingfisher Publications Plc 1992

ISBN 1 85697 264 X

Phototypeset by Waveney Typesetters, Norwich
Printed in China

MY FIRST ENCYCLOPEDIA

People
Long Ago

Kingfisher

Authors
Dominique Joly and Christopher Maynard

History consultant
Sally Purkis

Series consultant
Brian Williams

Editor
Odette Dénommée

Designer
Anne Boyer

Illustrators
Louis R. Galante
Marc Lagarde
Florence McKenzie
Barry Mitchell
François Pichon,
Etienne Souppart
Valérie Stetten

What is history?

History is about what took place and how people lived long ago. People who study history are called historians and archaeologists.

Just like detectives, historians and archaeologists hunt for clues to the way people once lived. Bits of pottery, old monuments, weapons, written records – these all tell us about the past.

Then, very patiently, historians and archaeologists put the different bits and pieces together like a giant jigsaw puzzle. It is thanks to them that we know about the people and the events this book describes.

When an historical site is discovered, archaeologists uncover and record everything they find. Pieces of pottery and beautifully carved stones may have bee lying buried for hundreds of years and must be dug out, slowly and gently. This picture shows archaeologists at work about 80 years ago.

FRAGILE

CONTENTS

THE MIDDLE AGES

 AROUND THE WORLD

TIMES OF CHANGE

THE INDUSTRIAL AGE

TODAY

Prehistory

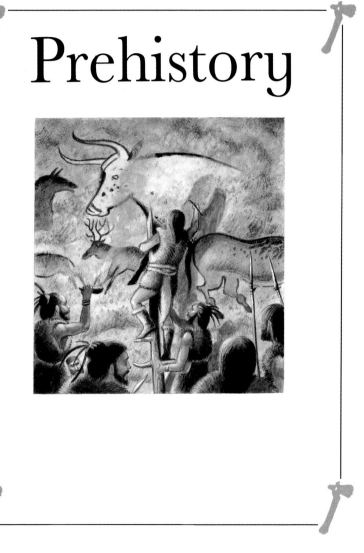

The first people

Human beings gradually grew taller

The first people appeared about two million years ago. They did not wear any clothes and lived in small groups. Some lived in caves, while others lived in simple shelters.

he first humans
arned how to
ake fire and how
 make simple tools
t of stone. They
ed these tools to
nt animals and to
op their food.

tools used by
the first people

⫟ Wandering hunters

Early people lived by
hunting. They had to
roam far and wide to
find the animals and
plants that were their
food. They made
shelters from branches
covered with animal skins.
These were easy to put up and
take down every time they moved on.

lamp

needle

Once early people had learned to control
fire, life was easier.

spearhead

rly people used bone needles to make clothes t of animal skins. A spear with a bone earhead made a good hunting weapon.

Village life

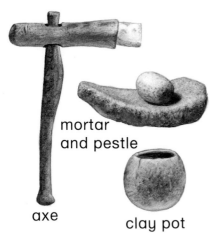

mortar
and pestle

axe

clay pot

A mortar and pestle
were used to grind
grain.

About 10,000 yea
ago, people begar
to keep flocks of
animals and to fa
the land. This gav
them a steady
supply of food an
wool. Now they
didn't have to roc
around all the tim
to find their food.

storians
ieve that
nt circles
stones like
s one were
ilt for religious
emonies. You can
the remains of these circles
places such as Stonehenge in England.

stead, people began to settle in small
lages. They wove wool to make clothes
d made bowls out of clay, which they
rdened in a fire. Their tools were made of
od, stone and bone. Later, they learned to
ke tools out of metal.

Amazing facts

No human being ever saw a dinosaur. Dinosaurs had vanished from the Earth many millions of years before the first people appeared.

Historians think the first people lived in Africa about two million years ago.

It takes about 100 taps to put a sharp edge on a stone chopper. This was the tool that the first people used for most jobs.

Some of the early people were skilled artists. They painted pictures of animals and hunting scenes on the walls of caves.

One of the first animals to live with humans was the dog. Wild dogs used to hang around settlements to get scraps of food, so some people think it was dogs who adopted humans, rather than humans who adopted dogs.

The Ancient

World

🏛 A merchant's notebook

In a land called Mesopotamia, in the Middle East, people settled and built the first cities in the world. Merchants came into the cities to trade their goods.

a merchant's clay tablet

The merchants kept records of what they traded by making marks on clay tablet. This is how writing first began, more th 5,000 years ago.

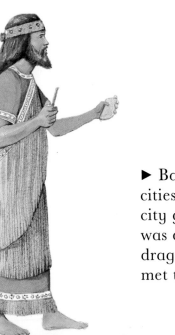

▶ Babylon was one of the gre cities in Mesopotamia. The m city gate, called the Ishtar Ga was decorated with pictures of dragons and bulls. Here, peop met to talk and trade.

🏛 Ancient Egypt

Most of Egypt is desert, but one of the greatest rivers in the world, the Nile, runs through it. Once a year, the Nile flooded its banks, leaving behind a layer of rich soil. Here the Egyptians settled. Their empire lasted for almost 3,000 years.

gyptian farmers dug irrigation channels to
ring water from the river to their fields.
here, they grew wheat and barley to make
ead and beer, and flax to weave into cloth.
om the marshes they gathered a reed
lled papyrus. They wove this to make
any useful things, such as rafts, sandals
d paper.

Pharaohs and gods

Some Egyptian gods

Horus   Isis   Osiris   Re'   Anubis

The Egyptians believed in many gods. The
also believed that their ruler, the pharaoh,
was a god. When he died, he was buried
with piles of treasure in a huge pyramid
or in a great tomb cut into a cliff.

his gold mask covered the
eserved body, or mummy,
Pharaoh Tutankhamun.
ae piles of treasure buried
th him were for him to
joy in the next world.

pyramid

The Hebrews

The Hebrews were a tribe of people from the area between Egypt and Mesopotamia. They were nomads who moved around with their flocks of sheep and goats. After hundreds of years of wandering, they settled and formed the Kingdom of Israel.

he Hebrews worshipped only one god.
1e laws of their god were written on tablets
stone. These heavy tablets were kept in
box called the Ark of the Covenant,
1ich the Hebrews took wherever
2y went.

🏛 Ancient India

In Ancient India, not everyone had the sam
religion. One group, the Hindus, believed
that the River Ganges was a holy river.
They came to bathe in it to wash away
their sins. They also came to worship their
different gods in temples decorated with
many statues. Hinduism is still the main
religion in modern India.

nother religious group in India was the
uddhists. Buddhism was founded by a
n called Siddhartha Gautama about
500 years ago. Siddhartha Gautama
s inspired with his ideas while he was
editating under a fig tree.

⚜ Sailing by the stars

The Polynesians were some of the greatest
sailors of all time. More than 3,000 years
ago, they were already sailing across the
huge Pacific Ocean in their catamarans to
find new islands to settle. They steered
by reading the stars, and by watching
the waves, the currents and
changes in
the wind.

Some Polynesian
people tattooed
their faces.

⚏ Ancient Greece

In Greece, a land of mountains, go
farmland was rare, but the sea was never f
away. The Ancient Greeks became gr
sailors and traders. They travelled f
and wide to trade their wine, o
pottery and jewellery f
wheat, wood, ivo
...almost anythi

out 2,500 years ago, Athens was
e richest Greek city of all.
famous temple, the
rthenon, stood
 gh above the
y and its busy
arket-place.

♨ The first Olympic Gam

Like the Egyptians, the Greeks had many gods. They held big festivals to honour the The mightiest of all the gods was Zeus. Special games were held at Olympia every four years in his honour. Here, the best athletes competed in different events. These were the very first Olympic Games.

A crown of olive leaves was awarded to the best athlete.

Throwing the discus and the race in armour were two of the events in the ancient Olympics.

Athena
Zeus
Poseidon
Apollo

Some Greek gods

mask

Stories about the gods were told in plays that sometimes lasted from dawn to dusk. In Greek theatres, the actors wore masks. The audience sat on stone seats, looking down on the stage.

🏛 The Roman Empire

About 1,800 years ag
the city of Rome was t
centre of the biggest empire anyone h
ever known. Roman soldiers had conquer
large parts of Europe and North Afric

hen the victorious army returned to Rome,
marched through the city to show off all
e riches that it had captured.
herever they went, the Romans built
g, stone-paved roads to link up the
ferent parts of their empire.

🏛 Life in Rome

Rome was the greatest city of its time. At it
biggest, it had almost one million inhabitant

In the centre of the city was an open area
called the Forum. The Forum was ringed b
monuments: temples, statues, columns and
splendid arches. Here, the citizens of Rome
met to chat and to do business.

A slave helped a noble boy wash and dress.

At school he wrote his lessons on wax tablets.

Afterwards he could play with a hoop or knuckle-bones.

In the afternoon he might go to the public baths with his father.

⚖ Christianity

The Romans believed in many gods, but n[ot]
all the people in their empire had the sam[e]
religion. In Palestine, in the easter[n]
part of the empire, a m[an]
called Jesus invite[d]
people to follo[w]
his belie[fs]

dove

any people decided
 follow Jesus'
achings and became
hristians. Slowly,
hristianity spread
rough the Roman
npire. At first it was
nned. But in the
d, most people in
e Empire became
ristians.

Some early Christian symbols

lamb

fish

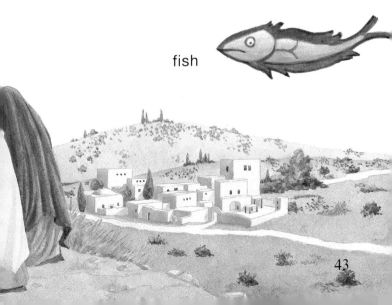

43

Amazing facts

About 70 years ago, the unopened tomb of the Egyptian pharaoh, Tutankhamun, was discovered. The treasures inside helped scientists and historians get a better idea of how the Ancient Egyptians lived.

People first started using coins about 2,700 years ago. Before that, traders exchanged goods. This was called bartering.

The Roman idea of entertainment was often very violent. At the Colosseum in Rome, as many as 100,000 people came to watch armed men called gladiators fight to the death. The floor of the Colosseum could also be flooded with water for mock sea battles and other spectacles.

The Middle

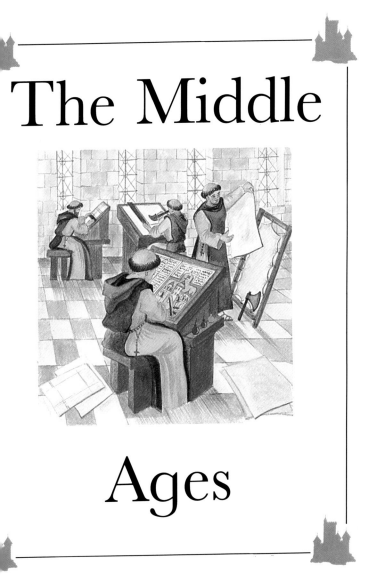

Ages

The invaders

Huns

At the height of its power, the Roman Empire stretched from Great Britain across Europe as far as the Middle East.

Angles

But many tribes of invaders kept attacking the Empire from the north and east. The Romans called these invaders barbarians.

Germans

After a time, the Roman Empire was defeated and split up into smaller kingdoms.

The barbarians mixed with the people of the old Empire.

Franks

The barbarians brought with them their own customs, laws and their skills in metalwork.

Visigoths

The Queen of Cities

Part of the Roman Empire survived in the east. Its capital was Constantinople (now called Istanbul). Here, merchants from the Far East, Europe and Africa met to trade and Constantinople soon became a very rich city. It was known as 'The Queen of Cities'.

nstantinople was
otected by high
ne walls. Inside,
re were beautiful
aces and a great
hedral topped by
lome. The city's
ftsmen were
nous for their
ldings and
rks of art.

Mosaics, like this
one of the Empress
Theodora, were
made of tiny bits of
coloured glass.

 # The Muslims

In Arabia, the prophet Muhammad, found
the religion called Islam. Many Arabs
became followers of Islam, or Muslims.
When Muslim warriors invaded North Afri
and Spain, they took their religion with the

herever they went, the Muslims built
sques where they could pray to their god,
ah. Their cities became centres of
rning, for they were great scientists and
re skilled in medicine and astronomy.

51

The Vikings

In the cold lands of the north lived the
Vikings. Most Vikings were farmers, but the
were also fierce warriors who raided the
coasts of Europe. They could row and sail
great distances in their light, flat-bottomed
ships, called longships.

any Vikings set out
search of new
rmland. They
ttled in France,
eland, Scotland and
e north of England.
e Vikings were also skilled
aftsmen and their ships were
ten decorated with beautiful
rvings like this one.

prow of a
Viking ship

Castles of stone

In Europe, in the Middle Ages, there were many wars, so landowners called lords live with their families and soldiers in castles. The first castles were built of wood. Later, they were made of stone with a deep ditch, or moat, all the way around the outside.

The peasants who farmed the lord's land lived in villages nearby. But in times of danger, they came into the castle for protection.

In wartime, soldiers stood guard in towers spaced along the castle wall.

Knights in armour

A lord had many soldiers called knights to serve him if he went to war. In peacetime, the knights needed to keep in training. Sometimes they travelled to tournaments, where they could take part in mock battles and compete against each other in jousts.

knight's training started early. At 6, he learned
ride and shoot. At 14, he became a squire and
rned how to fight. At 18, he became a knight.

 The Church

In Europe, in the Middle Ages, the Christian Church was very rich and powerful. Unlike most people, monks and nuns could read and write. They copied out books by hand and decorated them with illustrations. Monks and nuns were the only teachers too, but few people went to school.

► Kings and Church leaders spent a lot of money building great cathedrals. Thousands of craftsmen came from far and wide work on them.

59

Bustling towns

ost European towns about this time were
rounded by high stone walls. But inside,
arly all the buildings were made of wood.

e narrow, muddy streets were crowded with
ded carts, and cows, sheep and pigs on
ir way to market. Shops and workshops
ened straight onto the street. Shops that
sold the same goods were grouped
together in the same part of town.

Amazing facts

A knight's armour weighed about as much as a ten-year-old child. On top of the he also had to carry a heavy sword and shield.

People did not eat off plates or use fork in the Middle Ages. Instead, they used thei fingers to eat. The food was served on long slabs of bread.

Houses in the Middle Ages were dark and gloomy. Windows were tiny and were covered over with oiled paper. Glass windows were too expensive.

It took the wood of 8,000 oak trees to build even a small castle.

Around the

world

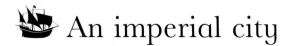

Outside Europe, other empires had developed. Emperors ruled over a great empire in China. In 1421, the emperor moved his court to the city of Beijing. He lived with his family and thousands of servants in a walled palace as big as a tow

e palace was called the Forbidden City,
cause no-one except the emperor's
usehold was allowed inside. In the streets
Beijing, craftsmen wove silk cloth and
inted porcelain bowls. China was famous
its silk and porcelain.

Warriors of Japan

In Japan, about 400 years
ago, fierce warriors called
samurai served their
overlords by fighting
in their wars.
To protect them in
battle, the samurai
wore armour made of
metal plates and leather.

pan was not just a country of war. It had
ny beautiful ceremonies and traditions
. One of these was the tea ceremony.
ople wore special robes and followed
ict rules for this
emony.

🚢 The Oba of Benin

The Benin people were famous for their sculpture.

About 500 years ago, Benin was one of the most powerful kingdoms in Africa. Its peop worshipped their king, the oba, as if he wer a god. The oba owned all the land in the country and his word was law.

Every year, for three months, the oba travelled around with his chiefs, dressed in his rich royal robes.
All kinds of ceremonies were held during this time.

 An Aztec city

In America, two great empires had developed. The Incas lived in what is now Peru, in South America. In what is now Mexico, the Aztecs ruled over a great kingdom from their capital, Tenochtitlán.

Girls prepare incense for a ceremony.

Tenochtitlán was built on islands in the middle of a marshy lake. Canals criss-crossed the city. In the centre stood great pyramid-shaped temples where priests performed ceremonies for the Aztec gods.

Priests were often teachers too. Here, a priest teaches children to play musical instruments.

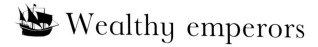 # Wealthy emperors

About 450 years ago, horsemen from the
north invaded India and founded the Mogul
Empire. The Mogul emperors lived in
beautiful palaces topped with golden domes.
Their gardens were filled with fruit trees and
splashing fountains.

he greatest Mogul emperor was Akbar.
kbar invited many artists and musicians to
 court to work for him. Akbar was a wise
d just ruler. He was a Muslim, but he
owed the many Hindus in his empire to
orship their gods as they wished.

Amazing facts

The Great Wall of China was built mo
than 2,000 years ago to protect China fron
invaders. It measures nearly 6,400 kilometr
and is the longest wall ever built.

In Japan, everyone had to show respect
to a samurai warrior, otherwise he could ki
you on the spot!

The words avocado, chocolate and
tomato all come from the Náhuatl languag
This was the language spoken by the Aztec
more than 500 years ago.

The Mogul emperor, Shah Jahan, love
his wife so much that, when she died, he bu
a beautiful building in white marble over h
grave. The building was the Taj Mahal.

Times of

change

 # New ideas

Around 1450, people in Europe started to take a great interest in learning. They studied the world they lived in and made important discoveries in science and astronomy. Artists also found new ways of showing what they saw around them.

e new ideas and knowledge spread
ckly, helped by the invention of printing.
ple felt as if a new age had begun.
at is why this period is often called the
naissance – Renaissance is a French word
t means rebirth.

🔭 European explorers

The new
ideas of the
Renaissance
also led to
an interest in
exploration.

cara

Better sailing ships and new instruments fo
navigating meant that sailors were able to

make longer voyages.
Kings and queens
encouraged explorers
go and discover new
lands and riches.
Europeans sailed to
Africa, India, the We:
Indies and America fo
the first time.

...ropean explorers used ...w kinds of sailing ships ...ch as the caravel, the ...rrack and the nao for ...ir long ocean ...yages.

nao

...rrack

🔭 Kings and queens

Elizabeth the First,
Queen of England

At this time, most of the countries of Europ
were ruled by kings and queens. Kings and
queens had almost complete power over th
countries.

The kings and queens of Europe built elegant new palaces for themselves and their courts. Philip the Second of Spain built a great palace called the Escorial outside his capital, Madrid.

Philip the Second, King of Spain

Louis the Fourteenth, King of France

But perhaps the grandest palace of all was Versailles, home of the French king, Louis the Fourteenth.

 Moscow

In Russia, the king was called the tsar. He lived in the capital, Moscow. The heart of Moscow, called the Kremlin, was surrounded by a wall. The most beautiful buildings, including the tsar's palace and several churches, were inside the Kremlin.

utside the Kremlin walls, the ordinary
ople lived in houses built of logs. These
oden houses caught fire easily. Sometimes
e spread from house to house so quickly
t half the city went up in flames.

Settlers in North Americ

More than 350 yea
ago, a group of
people from Englar
landed in North
America to settle
there. They were n
the first people to l
in North America.
Tribes of Native
Americans had bee
living there for
thousands of years.

e settlers farmed the land and traded with
Native Americans for furs. Over the
ars their farms grew. Ships filled with
od, tobacco and sugar from their farms
led across to Europe.

hough the settlers lived so far away,
y were still ruled by the King
England and had
pay him taxes.

War of Independence

As time went by, the settle
in North America
longer wanted to p
taxes to the King
Englar

To protest agai
a tax on to
settlers (weari
disguises) raid
three Engl
ships
Bost
Harbo
and threw th
cargo of
overboa

TEA

his was a signal for other settlers to join a volt. After six years of fighting, the English were defeated and the settlers became independent. A new country was born; it was called the United States of America. People across the new country celebrated their victory by parading behind their new flag.

 # Slavery

The European settlers
in America needed
many workers to farm thei
crops of cotton, tobacco,
sugar cane and rice. This l
to a huge trade in slaves
from Africa.

ople were captured on the west coast of
rica, then chained up in ships and taken
America. There they were sold as slaves.
any of them died on the way.

er the years, about 15 million Africans
re shipped to North and South America
fore slavery was finally banned and all
slaves set free.

Australia

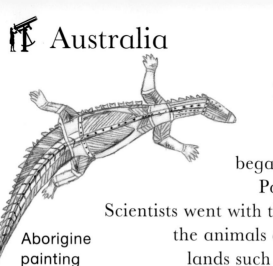

In the 170[0]
Europe[an]
explor[ers]
began to map t[he]
Pacific Oce[an.]
Scientists went with them to stu[dy]
the animals and plants [of]
lands such as Austral[ia.]

Aborigine
painting

Tribes of Aborigines had already been livin[g]
in Australia for thousands of years. They
hunted animals for food and were skilled
painters. At celebrations they danced to
music played on a long wooden flute.

The French Revolution

on after the settlers in North America had
ined their independence, the people of
ance rose up against their king, Louis the
teenth. Under his rule, the poor had
come even poorer and many people didn't
ve enough food to eat.

In 1789, in Paris, a crowd
attacked a prison called the
Bastille and the revolution
began. The king was
executed and the new
government passed laws to
give equal rights
to everyone.

Amazing facts

Leonardo da Vinci was a great all-round genius of the Renaissance. He was a painter, sculptor, architect, engineer, scientist and mathematician.

Christopher Columbus sailed to America in 1492. But he believed he had travelled to the East Indies and was somewhere near Japan.

Louis the Fourteenth, King of France, ruled his country for longer than any other king or queen in Europe. He came to the throne when he was only five years old and ruled for 72 years.

The city of New York stands on the island of Manhattan. In 1626, a group of Dutch settlers bought the small island from a tribe of Native Americans for a chest of beads, some cloth and other trinkets.

The

ndustrial age

Coal and steam

About 200 years ago, machin[es]
powered by steam changed t[he]
way people lived and worke[d].
Instead of farmi[ng]
and working in th[eir]
homes, peo[ple]
moved into t[he]
towns to work [in]
factories. This w[as]
the start of t[he]
Industr[ial]
Revolutio[n].

The new machines burned lots of coal.
Thousands of workers, including children,
spent long days down the mines digging o[ut]
the coal. At the surface, women sorted the
coal into baskets and sacks. Mining
was hard, dirty and often
dangerous work.

🏭 The pioneers

The pioneers were men and women who left their homes on the east coast of North America to settle in the Far West. Groups of as many as 100 families set out together in wooden wagons hauled by oxen or horses.

fore finding their new
mes, the pioneers had
face many dangers.
any of them died of
nger, drought and
ezing cold. Others were attacked by
tive Americans, who didn't want strangers
settle on their hunting grounds.

Steam trains

Locomotives powered by steam pulled the first trains. Tunnels and bridges were built take the new trains through hills and over rivers. Now people and goods could be moved about faster and more cheaply.

1869, the first railway to cross the United tes of America from east coast to west st was finished. The new railway brought usands more people out to the West and ped settle this huge land.

101

Cars and planes

After the steam engine came the internal combustion engine. The internal combustion engine ran on petrol or diesel. This was the engine that drove cars and trucks, and powered the first aeroplanes.

The first cars didn't look much like modern cars and were very hard to drive. But by 1900, cars looked more like they do today. New air-filled tyres made them more comfortable and some cars could reach speeds of up to 130 kilometres an hour.

About the same time, the first aeroplanes took to the air. The Wright brothers flew the first aeroplane in 1903. In 1927, Charles Lindbergh was the first person to fly alone across the Atlantic Ocean.

 World War I

In 1914, a great war broke out that lasted for four years. Many different countries we dragged into the war, which was called World War I.

During the war, soldiers fought from trenches that they had dug in the ground. By the end of the war, millions of soldiers had been killed.

Women played a very important part in th war. Many worked on farms and in factori while the men were away fighting. In the years after the war, women fought for and won the right to vote and to carry on working.

fe in the trenches was very hard. When it
ined, the trenches became damp and muddy.
any soldiers got diseases such as trench foot
m always wearing wet boots and socks.

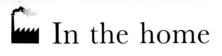

In the home

ew inventions
began to make
everyday life much
easier. Some houses
had hot and cold
running water,
and electric lighting
became more common.
People listened to the first
radios, and telephones
allowed them to talk to
each other across long distances.

In many countries, children could now go to
school to learn to read, write and count.
New discoveries in medicine meant that
doctors were able to cure diseases that had
once killed thousands of people.

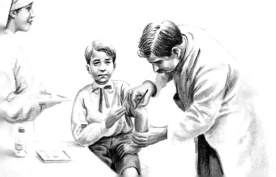

Revolution in Russia

In Russia, many people were unhappy with the way the tsar ruled the country. In 1917, a great crowd of workers and soldiers marched to protest against food shortages.

the revolution that followed, the tsar
dicated and the Communist Party came
power under their leader, Lenin. The
mmunists wanted to set up a fairer system
government. In the name of the Russian
ople, they took control of most of the land,
operty and factories in the country.

World War II

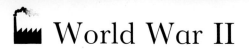

In 1939, a second great war broke out that
spread to almost every part of the world.
This was World War II.

World War II was fought in Europe, in
North Africa and in South-East Asia.
In Europe, aeroplanes were used to bomb
many cities, destroying millions of building
and killing hundreds of thousands of peopl

The war finally ended in 1945, when the
first nuclear bombs were dropped on the
Japanese towns of Hiroshima and Nagasak

▶ Powerful searchlights were used to pick out
enemy aeroplanes as they flew over a city.
Sirens blared and people ran for cover in
air raid shelters.

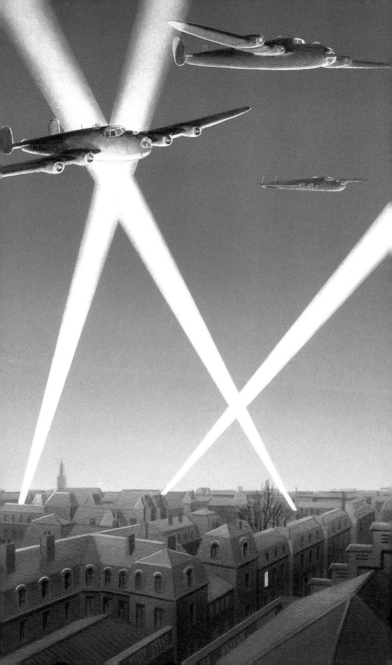

Amazing facts

About 140 years ago, a tailor in San Francisco started making hard-wearing trousers for gold miners in California. His name was Levi Strauss and his trousers became known as jeans.

For many poor people living in Europe the United States of America offered the possibility of a new and better life. Between 1830 and 1910, about 28 million European sailed to the United States.

Thomas Edison was a famous America inventor who invented the phonograph: a machine that could play back recorded human voices. But his most important invention of all was probably the electric light bulb.

Today

The United Nations

After World War II, an organization was s
up to help keep peace in the world. It was
called the United Nations, or UN. Since
then, the UN has been a place where all th
countries of the world can meet and talk to
one another. The UN also gives advice and
money to help poorer countries improve
their people's health and education.

Exploring Space

For thousands of years people had wondere
what lay out in Space. In 1957, the first
space probe, *Sputnik 1*, was launched into
Space and circled around the Earth. Then
1969, two astronauts landed on the Moon f
the first time.

tronauts can now
e and work in space
itions for
eks at a time.
ientists have
eady sent
ace probes to
id on Mars
d Venus.

Satellites out in
Space send
telephone and
television signals all
around the world.

New inventions

Ever since the first people discovered how
make stone tools, human beings have been
inventing things that have changed the wa
they live.

Today, we can fly around the world in just one and a half days, while computers and machines do much of our work for us. And people are still inventing new things. What will we come up with next?

Amazing facts

Since 1945, many new nations have be
formed. There are now over 190 nations in
the world.

The Hubble Space Telescope is the
biggest telescope in Space. This powerful
telescope can send us pictures of stars and
galaxies that cannot be seen by telescopes
the Earth.

In the last 100 years, there have been
more developments in science and
technology than in the previous 4,000 year

INDEX